It's a Fruit, It's a Vegetable, It's a Pumpkin

By Allan Fowler

Consultants

Robert L. Hillerich, Professor Emeritus,
Bowling Green State University, Bowling Green, Ohio;
Consultant, Pinellas County Schools, Florida

Lynne Kepler, Educational Consultant

Fay Robinson, Child Development Specialist

CHILDRENS PRESS®
CHICAGO

Design by Herman Adler Design Group
Photo Research by Feldman & Associates, Inc.

Library of Congress Cataloging-in-Publication Data

Fowler, Allan.
    It's a fruit, it's a vegetable, it's a pumpkin / by Allan Fowler.
    p. cm. – (Rookie read-about science)
    ISBN 0-516-06039-2
    1. Pumpkin—Juvenile literature. [1. Pumpkin.] I. Title.
  II. Series.
SB347.F68   1995
641.3'562–dc20
                                  95-5565
                                      CIP
                                      AC

What's the biggest
fruit or vegetable
you can think of?

A watermelon may be hard to lift. But pumpkins grow even bigger. A pumpkin could weigh as much as 800 pounds!

Farmers show off their
biggest pumpkins at county
fairs or state fairs.

Pumpkins grow on vines.
A vine is a plant that
doesn't stand up by itself.

Some vines cling to walls
or trees or posts.

7

The vines that bear large fruits or vegetables, like pumpkins, grow along the ground.

Melons and cucumbers, zucchini and gourds also grow on vines.

Is a pumpkin a fruit or a vegetable? Botanists — scientists who study plants — tell us that a pumpkin is a fruit.

You might think of it
as fruit when you eat
pumpkin pie.

But pumpkin is also served
as a vegetable, or is made
into soup.

In fact, a pumpkin is really
a kind of squash. And
most people call squash
a vegetable.

Among the first people
to raise pumpkins were
Native Americans.

Pumpkins were eaten at
the first Thanksgiving feast
by the Pilgrims in 1621.

Today, pumpkin pie is a favorite dessert, especially with Thanksgiving dinner.

There's one time of year
when you see pumpkins
everywhere — Halloween.

Halloween pumpkins
have faces, and are
called jack-o'-lanterns.

You see grinning jack-o'-lanterns in windows if you go trick-or-treating.

You see them at Halloween parties, along with goblins and skeletons, bats and black cats.

To make a jack-o'-lantern,
draw eyes, a nose, and a
mouth on a pumpkin shell
for a grown-up to cut out.

Then scoop out the
pumpkin until it is hollow.

People used to put lighted
candles inside jack-o'-
lanterns. But it's not a good
idea to do that, because
a candle can start a fire.
A flashlight is much safer.

If a pumpkin is too small to
be carved, you can still make
a jack-o'-lantern out of it.

Just paint a spooky face on the pumpkin. Spooky — but in a funny way.

You wouldn't want to scare your friends and family.

Or would you?

Words You Know

jack-o-lanterns

pumpkin pie

vines

30

pumpkin

watermelon

squash

cucumber

Index

botanists, 12
candles, 26
carving (pumpkins), 24-25, 27
cucumbers, 10
faces (on jack-o'-lanterns), 21-22, 24, 29
fairs, 5
farmers, 5
flashlight, 26
fruits, 3, 9, 12-13
gourds, 10
Halloween, 21-22
jack-o'-lanterns, 21-22, 24-27, 29
melons, 10
Native Americans, 16
parties (Halloween), 22
pie (pumpkin), 13, 19
Pilgrims, 18
plants, 6, 12
soup, 14
squash, 15
Thanksgiving, 18-19
trick-or-treat, 22
vegetables, 3, 9, 12, 14-15
vines, 6, 9-10
watermelons, 4
zucchini, 10

About the Author

Allan Fowler is a free-lance writer with a background in advertising. Born in New York, he lives in Chicago now and enjoys traveling.

Photo Credits